THE **POWER** WITHIN, A *Woman's* WORTH:

FROM BOTH SEXES

EXTENDED VERSION 2ND EDITION: Introducing the 5 Laws of Harnessing Your Worth

AARON JORDAN, JR.

Aaron Jordan focuses on bringing holistic inspiration to the literary world. All stories are not meant to depict, portray, or represent a person or place. Religious notations mentioned are not to defame or negate any other religion.

ISBN: 978-1546910930
Cover Design: Vintage Media Solutions
Layout Design: Write On Promotions

DEDICATION

I would like to dedicate this book to two very important people in my life, first, is my beloved wife; Ashley Jordan. You are the CEO of our family's legacy and the fire that ignite our flame. She has given me so much strength in my time of weakness and pushed me to keep going even when I was ready to throw in the towel. May 7, 2013 my creator blessed me with opportunity to confess my love to my forever and can spend the rest of my life with my God's Gift. She has blessed me with a life of laughter even through the times of hardships, supported me even when I did not have a dime to my name, and nurtured me with her warming spirit. For this I am eternally grateful and want to spend the rest of my life striving to continue to keep a smile on your face.

Yours Truly,
Your Husband,
Forever in Love

The second person I would like to dedicate this book to; she is my heart, my princess, and daughter, Teanna R. Jordan. On a cold winter day in 2005, my world changed for the better. Changing me and my mindset; December 2005, on a Friday at 10:53p I was blessed with a 6lb 3oz baby girl. One of the purposes of dedicating this book to my daughter is to show her that you should never give up on your goals and dreams to be great and inspire. Anything is possible, even when life deals you a bad hand; our creator never leaves you nor forsake you.

Love,

Daddy

Table of Contents

Introduction

I was sitting in the Nashville International Airport one evening just thinking about everything that has taken place in my life over the last twenty-four months; as I was in deep thought I got a call to my cell phone, well it rung several times, people calling congratulating me on the accomplishment of my first book etc. But, out of those calls there was one that touched me and solidified my mission in writing this book and opened my eyes that much greater; the young woman stated to me after I said hello, "Greetings Mr. Jordan, you don't know me but we know a mutual friend and I got your number from him hope you don't mind?" About six weeks ago I was in a very bad space mentally and emotionally in regard to my relationship of 4 years and our mutual friend suggested that I read your book; so, I proceeded to your website that he gave me to purchase a copy, but, in my first mind I did have some reservations about it because I didn't trust the whole relationship book cliché. But, I went with my gut and purchased your book."

At that moment of the conversation I gave her my deepest appreciation for her support, but she continued to speak as if it was her mission or assignment to reach out to me in this type of gratitude. The young woman continued saying, "I went with my gut and purchased your book, it arrived at my office about week or so later from the time that I ordered from your site. I was very excited to read but I still had my reservations so it sat in my desk for about another week after it came to my office. A couple of days after that our mutual friend contacted me and asked to do lunch; then he asked if I ordered your book and have I read it yet. I told him that I had reservations about reading it so it is sitting in the top draw of my desk here at the office; he urged me with the utmost sincerity in his voice to read your book. So, as I was about to leave the office that evening, I took your book out of the top draw of my desk and sat down to read your introduction and first chapter to see if this was worth taking home to read over a glass of wine or was it a wasted suggestion from a friend. Mr. Jordan as I began to read your book, I found myself trapped and stuck in my office for the next couple of hours reading your words. It drew me in to the point of me crying and amazed that it seemed like you wrote out my whole life situation in regards to dating. I just wanted you to know personally from me how your book has enhanced me with the knowledge and the understanding of me again, you changed my life!"

After hearing this young woman's story and the sincerity in her gratitude, tears began to flow down my face; not tears of sadness, but the tears of joy. Simply because, from the words that God gave me it has truly touched the life of another person. As I broke my silence on the phone, the only thing that could come out of my mouth as a response to the young woman was "WOW!" She laughs but, after hearing her story and how she had her reservations then proceeds to read my book a few days after she ordered it and it came to her office got to me and solidified this series and my passion in this space. Often, I get ask the question, "Are you a doctor?" or "What degrees or schooling do you have to speak on Relationships?" Everything that I write about I have been through and then some, my gift of observations and the opportunity to help countless of people with their relationships deems me capable to speak and help in this space. My analogies and philosophies are broken down to the point of understanding by any person.

On countless occasions, I hear people saying that they are ready for true love and true happiness when it pertains to dating and having a successful relationship, that it baffles me. People want what I call the "Fairy Tale" instead of the "Total Bliss." People will not be taken seriously in finding love until they take themselves seriously in this regard. Meaning, that until you get to the deepest root of your greatest project in life, which is you; your love life will continue to be a constant cycle of pain, hurt, and deceit. Harnessing your true worth and capabilities in this realm and spectrum of your life in dating could seriously weed out those deep seeded roots that have been planted in your life from your past, before you ever had a love life.

As I look out of my eye gates at the countless things we as men and women settle for when it comes to dating and relationships, it is astonishing. How women continue to devalue themselves and their morals just for the sake of having a warm body lay next to them at night, also how we as men still think that we are pulling the wool over women eyes when we do the things we do or the deceit that we carry in our relationships; we are only fooling ourselves. Women always remember that your worth is undeniable and your value is priceless; you are more than what you settle for and you deserve more than what you think you deserve. Men we are leaders and conquerors of the land and the cultivators of women; we were predestined for greatness, our role as a man is much greater than the stereotypes that has been place on us as a man.

Understand that in dating and relationship, as stated before, you will not be taken seriously in your love life unless you become serious within yourself and get to the deepest root of your life's greatest project, which is you. Meaning, to have the level of success in your relationship or to find your God's Gift, you must be prepared and ready to receive him/her with open arms; getting rid of the life consuming baggage that you have been carrying around with you for years. Not being able to let go of the things that caused you the most hurt and pain physically, mentally, and emotionally can truly sabotage your love life progression from being one the most meaningful experiences of your life. In this continuation series of part one, "The Power Within, A Women's Worth: From Both Sexes", this will give you a much deeper and greater understanding of what your true worth and value is when it comes to dating and relationships. People think that they understand the dynamics of this genre, but it is on a much greater scale than what individuals' minds can fathom. In my professional opinion, the surface is not even being scratched with some of the professionals in this space helping people to understand the dynamics of what it means to have a successful meaningful relationship; not stating that every relationship is going to be picture perfect and is going to last a lifetime. But, what I am saying is that if you are truly serious about your love life and making peace within yourself of the baggage that you carry from each relationship or dating experience that you have, you must be able to deal with what is facing you in the mirror and not run from that person to try mask your hurt; once that is mastered you will be able to grasp the concept of your worth that much greater. Meaning, that once you truly harness and take back ownership of your worth and value that was bruised from your passed relationships and experiences; you will begin to see what you are worth, what you truly must offer, and you will never doubt what you're truly called to be ever again. The words, actions, slanders, etc. that come from others will roll off you like water on a duck back. I want to share a story of purpose mixed with passion with you:

One evening as I was preparing for travels the following day a few years ago, I heard a voice that spoke to me so vividly and asked me one simple question, "Are You Ready?" I was shocked and stunned by the question, but not wanting seem like I was talking to myself; I brushed off what I heard and continued my preparation for my flight the next morning. But, again the voice spoke to me; this time in a like roar type tone demanding that I hear and I answer. Shaken and nervous now, I asked for what? In reply, a few minutes later, the voice spoke again and said, "For where I am about to take you?" At this point I was having a full-blown conversation with myself seemingly, but, at that moment I knew who I was talking to; my creator. The conversation ended with my creator saying, "Be Prepared for what is about to happen!" This experience took place October 2012, right after I wrote my first book entitled, The Power Within, A Women's Worth: From Both Sexes; but, knowing me I had questions that I was looking for to be answered about this experience. The voice did not return at that very moment when asking certain questions for answers, you would have thought I was one those guys sitting in a padded room talking to myself, so I continued and put together my first book tour that took place in January 2013 to 2-3 cities every other month out through that year. As I was in preparation for the tour I receive a phone call from someone and their lead in question to me was, "Are You Ready?"

This call instantly made me reflect on the encounter I had with my creator some month's prior, but I did not go into explaining that to whom it was that called at the time; I was just stunned and stuck for a minute. At this point, I am thinking to myself that this is the second time this question has come up on two different occasions; is there something that I am missing to receive my answer. I brushed off the question again and continued to move forward, anticipating an awesome first tour. Later that year, as I wrapped up the last city on this tour which was in Brooklyn, New York, I had the opportunity to speak and share my book at a Women's Shelter there three blocks from the Barclays Center in the heart of Brooklyn. That experience was so amazing and humbling that my whole outlook and outreach had changed at that very moment. But, that was not the most interesting thing that had taken place during that trip; after speaking and giving out a few free books to a couple of women in that shelter organization, there was this one lady that stood out to me. She was sitting in the back of the room, a few people popped in and out during this time of the speaking session; but as stated, this one lady popped in and sat in the back of the room listening.

As I finished speaking to the few that were in attendance, I held a Q&A portion for the audience at the end. At this point, the older mid-aged woman in the back got up and proceeded to walk toward the front of the room; while walking, she asked if she could ask me a question, I stated "Sure, this is the Q&A portion of the session!" She asked me, "How old are you?" now granted the thought that came into my mind was to be on guard and have my wall up, but I proceeded to tell her my age as my wife was probably thinking the same thing as I was thinking as she was walking up. But, as she begun to talk and proceed with her question I instantly had to internally ask for forgiveness; because as she started speaking, she left me kind of speechless. She stated, *"Sir, you are my sons age and I am floored by the appointed calling you have over your life. As I was getting off the elevator, I had no intentions of stopping in and participating, but, there was something telling me I had sit and listen to what you had to say. As you were speaking, there was a glow from the top of your head to your shoulders. Are you ready for where you are about to go? Be prepared cause you are going to bless a many of people with the words you speak!"* Instantly, my mind was blown and I thought cameras were about to come out from around the corner or some sorts; because this was now the third time I was hit with this experience and question of "Are you ready!". Saying that to say, that in life we are all birth with a purpose to carry out. However, we are in many ways distracted by life many obstacles and most of the time we get in our own way of our predestined divine purpose. Therefore, we wonder why our outcome in certain situations don't go as we planned them to go; oftentimes, in personal development one of our major hindering

factors are people around and the people we allow
to have an ordinance in our lives.

Chapter 1: "WHY"

"WHY", is one of the biggest questions among both men and women. This question usually comes about when displacement or confusion is in the picture or simply in general conversation in different social setting and etc. But most importantly this is the most asked question that gets answered over and over again but continually gets asked. For instance, "Why are men the way they are?" or "Why do women nitpick so much?" These questions then prove one thing and that is that "WHY" is never meant to be understood but yet observed. Meaning that once you observe your why in a situation dealing with the opposite sex, you then find yourself drawing out factual conclusions about the why factor. Observations are a key component that is missing in this 21st century realm of dating. This is one of the reasons the initial parts of dating are so disconnected and misunderstood.

Observations are truly something that can lead a person to finding everlasting happiness. Often times I have been asked the questions, "Why can't I ever find the right person?" or even "Why I am not appreciated in my relationship?" At one point and time I even asked myself those same questions. Everyone has been at that "WHY" point in their lives a few times over before. It took me a great deal of time to learn myself as a man and as an unbiased person to figure out the answer to these questions. The answer is simple, as stated before the why factor is not to be understood but yet observed. If both, a man or woman are in a supposedly committed relationship and they feel that they are not being shown the love that they are due. Then instead of getting frustrated and stressed in a sense just stop, breathe, and observe the situation to yourself. Observe yourself first on what you're doing **(basically a self-check)** and then observe your mate's actions, words, body language, and mostly importantly their eyes. For these are some of the basic elements that will help you draw out your factual conclusions to the "WHY" factor.

Following the observation method, a lot of your "WHY" questions would be answered to the point of you knowing how to better assess the situation. In my life thus far, I have truly experienced the meaning of this "WHY" factor being so evident. Personally, I have gone through the highs, lows, and let downs in this dating and/or relationship world. Through my experience, I have learned so many things and observed so many personal situations, that things are much clearer to me in a sense. Things, situations, and love go in stages. This is something that I call "The 4th Quarter Love". Meaning dating, relationships, and love in the beginning goes in 4 cycles. These cycles typically happen within the first 24 months if that long, but often gets repeated throughout relationships and marriages as well. Let's go in more depth of these 4 cycles:

Cycle 1: 90-day process

As stated before "WHY" is biggest question that takes place in today's dating and/or relationship realm but, it's also a part of the 1st cycle as well as the other 3 cycles. Observation is the greatest tool in this first cycle. Meaning this is the point of the relationship where each party observes each other and basically sees if this shall continue. During this process, this is when most people are deceived in seeing the truth about a person. This is the glam stages of a relationship, seeing without seeing the "REAL". The 1st cycle is where most would fall for the sweet smiles, gentle kisses, and sweet whispers in the ear. But often the motives and intentions are solely far from what it seems. A person during this process of the first cycle generally begins to reveal themselves after about 65 days. After that you begin to see the habits, character flaws, and etc in that person. From this point a person can see if this is something that he or she would want to pursue further. Most people confuse this cycle with sex. Meaning, most consider this 90-day process as strictly going without sex or the woman withholding herself from a man. This cycle could be just that, but, this cycle goes much deeper than just sex. As stated before observations are one of the most vital components in the dating and relationship arena. Through this cycle, the opportunity of evaluation is performed. Meaning that through this cycle you can use this process to evaluate yourself on how you are with the opposite sex. Most people try to skate through this cycle letting the good in the beginning or the first couple weeks cloud their judgment. Even mostly, they just don't want to see what the truth is. Your everlasting happiness should mean more to you than you sabotaging it for the beginning sweet nothings.

Cycle 2: Validation

Validation generally comes next in the 4-cycle process of dating, relationships, and love. This means that after you establish some things, boundaries, and make the decision that this might be something that you want to see where it goes. Either the man or woman begins to ask these questions, "How do you feel about us?" or they may even make it personal by asking "How do you feel about me?" Some ask these questions more frequently than others. But generally, when these questions are asked that means that this person needs validation for his or her affection. At some point this can cause a strain on the relationship and if asked all the time this shows a sign of insecurity. Often, people go through this moment or period of validation and not even realize their actions. But the truth is, everyone needs a little bit of validation when it comes to dating and relationships. But as stated before, in some cases it can cause a strain in a lot of areas. At this point of the relationship, some form of comfort should be established and both of your minds begin to wonder about the future of the two. Women please take heed and don't be deceived on thinking that when a man is with you at this stage of the relationship that we don't think about the future. That is not true by no means, the mindset of a man and woman are not far from the same because we desire the same things in a sense. The only difference is that women mindsets can be a bit more crafty and clever than ours. All these things involving the mindset fall under validation. Because at this point of the relationship your minds begin to wonder about a lot of things I like to call "What ifs." The "what if" factor brings about the number one question during this cycle as stated before, "How do you feel about us?" This begins the whole validation cycle.

Validation comes about for many reasons and certain instances. Whether it's coming from a *person giving affection, showing affection, or mainly needing the attention; all of these factors bring about the validation period. Example: If a man pursues a woman, initially in the beginning he is going to do everything in his power to show the woman of interest that she is appreciated and wanted. This is where the 90-day process of Observation is performed. He will court the woman of interest in several different ways: dinners, movies, flowers, and whatever else he can think of to show his interest and affection. After this is complete, he begins to wonder **(mind you this only works if the man/woman is genuinely interested in something long-term)** if this can go further to something long-term. Because all of his spare time, efforts, and energy is spent showing and giving this woman the time and attention she needs. He will ask that number one question that is asked during this period. The reason for him asking this question during this time is because he figures that if we are spending* this significant amount of time and energy with each other then, "What are we?"

These are the things that go on in the validation cycle. But, if validation is constantly needed in a sense then you have a few things that need to be discuss and made aware of. Because as stated before, constantly needing validation of affection can cause a strain on any type of relationship; that's why in this period ACTIONS demolishes the need for constant validation. Meaning that instead of a person constantly asking these questions, their actions should speak for themselves and that should validate how that person feels truly about you.

Cycle 3: Getting over past hurts

In this cycle, this is where the relationship or dating period is tested. Trust is a major component to the progression of a relationship or even dating. When it is broken, then it is often very *hard to regain that trust in a man or woman. During this process, this is where the seed of grudges begin to resurface. As stated in cycle two, men mindsets are not far from women when it comes to looking for love and wanting happiness. We want the same things in a sense and trust is one of those things. Often, it is very hard to trust someone with your heart. Because of past experiences and going through certain situations that caused a person to have a lot hurt. Finally getting to the point of trusting your heart with someone and getting to this process of the cycle is a plus for a person that has trust issues and insecurities. But because you got to this cycle doesn't mean that you are out of the woods yet. Because grudges were built from past hurts. During this third cycle, things begin to happen within a person especially if that person had a rocky past relationship or marriage. Sometimes depending on the person that you are dealing with, this particular cycle could happen a lot faster than the norm. Example: Things can be going so great* in the beginning stages of your relationship or dating process. Then something triggers old memories or past situations that you went through that caused you to be the way you are mentally. Those triggers could be anything such as: you were dealing with an insecure person that drove you to the breaking point, cheating, liars, and whatever else that caused you to have inward grudges. Dealing with these inward grudges head on and preferably before committing to someone, would actually save you a lot of unnecessary issues going forth.

Getting over your past hurts is much easier said than done. Also in this process, men and women do things differently but pretty much the same. Meaning that we have the same methods of getting through this process but go about doing them differently. Let's look at the fact of a person leaving one relationship and jumping back onto the dating scene or into another relationship within a short period of time. This will be discussed in greater detail later on throughout the book, but *briefly, this is one of the worst things a person can do to themselves and others. As stated before, this is a true test of a relationship in the beginning stages of the dating and relationship arena.*

Cycle 4: Decisions

The final cycle of what I call "The 4th Quarter Love" is Decisions. This may sound simple and plain but believe it or not this is a powerful tool to depict your happiness. At this point in your life most that gets to this cycle has achieved a great milestone. Because at this point in your life, once you have followed the process of observation you are in a position to control the direction of your love life fully. Meaning that by the time you have made it to this point truly followed the steps in observation, and evaluation when you look up anywhere from 12-24 months has past. Within that time frame, you have the power of decision making. Most would say that this is wedding bell stage and say "Let's go pick out a ring!" But with some people this sometimes leads to the wedding stages. At this particular cycle, this is where most people make some of the worst decisions in dating and relationships. Just like in cycle one, but in this cycle, it's a bit more detrimental to make a bad decision solely because this is where the spirit of regrets is formed. How, you ask! Let's go in more detail on this cycle.

Most would say regrets in dating and relationship comes at any stage of the relationship, I beg to differ! Regrets come when a person starts thinking that the grass is greener on the other side. Not knowing that they have all of what they need right in front of them, nothing more or less, but everything that they need to sustain fully in a committed relationship.

Many things can trigger individuals at this point to make bad decisions. Whether it is an argument on whatever the case may be. A person may feel like their partner is not showing them enough attention due to work, family issues, or etc.

So, the partners mind begins to wonder on how it would be if they went elsewhere to fill that particular void that they are feeling. Often times it is never what it may seem to be. Sometimes the person gets caught in trying to fill that void or they never get caught but it is eating away at their conscious. However, many would make the decision to leave at that point in the relationship. But then as a few months goes by they find themselves back at square one of the process having "REGRETS." Regretting the decision that they made, thinking that the grass is greener on the other side. Most people miss out on that shot of having true happiness on the first go around due to this cycle. Then find them searching the next few years or even decades for something that came remotely close to what they had before the "REGRETS." This in this case, was nothing more or nothing less than everything they initially wanted and needed to sustain in a relationship. Following the steps of observation and evaluation, getting to the point of confronting your past hurts to get to this last cycle is major. Being able to not bring about unnecessary regrets in your life and love life will make you that much happier.

Chapter 2: "Rebounding"

The healing process after every relationship is something that every person should take heed to. But often times they never do. Everyone has been at fault of this at some point in their life. Personally, I can truly relate to this as well. Not giving yourself enough time to heal and free yourself of that emotional bond, can cloud your judgment in many areas in dating. Any person in courtship that proceeds longer than 6 months, for whatever reason does not make it to the decision phase of that relationship, needs to take time to heal. But instead of doing so, we go through this "REBOUND PERIOD." Consequently, this is one of the worst periods to go through in dating. Going through this period and not giving yourself time to replenish your emotions and thought process, this sends you through a cycle I would like to call "2-wheel motion."

This cycle describes rebounding in a great deal. The 2-wheel motion cycle is simply a two-part roller coaster love cycle. Meaning that once you continue in this rebound period of your life and continue devaluing your worth, you will continue to have the same life results and constantly going in circles with your love life. Now granted some of the rebound relationships do last for quite some time, but only until you go through cycle 3 as stated before in Chapter 1. Not getting over past your hurts is what triggers the downfall of REBOUND relationships. This proves why this is so evident. Which also proves my philosophy of the 2-wheel motion cycle; under this cycle "Cloudy Judgment and Instant Consoling" are the two things that represent this analogy of the 2-wheel motion cycle. Let's go in more detail on the 2-wheel motion cycle:

Cycle 1: Cloudy Judgment

*When leaving one relationship without taking the proper precautions needed to heal mentally and emotionally, you put yourself in a tough limbo and certain things begin to happen. Without healing you begin to search for something to fill that void of companionship. Which granted nothing is wrong with that but the steps taken where out of sequence. This is where the start of rebound relationships begin and the evolution of cloudy judgment are started. How so you ask? Well, let's go in detail with this first cycle under the 2-wheel motion analysis. Assume that you have been in your relationship or marriage for 5-10yrs. Things have not been great for quite some time and the two of you decide to get a divorce or end the relationship. You're going through the process of finalizing your divorce or bringing closure to your relationship, (**Now this is where it gets tricky**) but in the process of that finalization or closure you* *meet someone. This person's vibe and ora is everything that you have been waiting for in companionship, so you think. Things are going great for awhile but, you didn't follow the steps of observation and evaluation. What you assumed was everything that you wanted is the same thing that you ended your 5-10yr relationship over. "Triggers", this is so evident in this cycle of what I call "2-wheel motion." Because you did not give yourself the time needed to truly heal properly, salvage your emotions, and mend your wounds or bond. You have jeopardized your judgment on being able to decipher between the BULL.*

At this point, most would be in denial about being this way mentally. But look at yourself and evaluate when was the last time you moved to another relationship or started dating before it was time for you to do so. Just think about that for a few seconds! What was the outcome of it? What was the outcome of you moving on before that vulnerable and cleansing state has truly passed? Most would say that after being in a relationship for so long, that after it's over they can just move on to get over the last, HA! That's why a lot of people experience some of the things that they go through. This is the reason being, because the proper steps and precautions were not being exemplified to get over certain things dating and relationship wise. I can truly attest to this, because even myself I have been at this particular cycle so many times before out through my life. We all have, but once the steps are properly taken and used seriously we can truly begin to have the type of relationship and dating experience we want. As stated in chapter 1, your happiness should mean more to you than you sabotaging it for the sweet nothings or what seems to be the real deal.

Cycle 2: Instant Consoling

Instant Consoling is the most common when it comes to the process of trying to get over a person. But, even though it is the most common it's also the deadliest emotional wise in this 2-wheel motion cycle. Reason being, is because you set yourself up to fail every time by you needing that instant gratification from the opposite sex. In this Instant Consoling cycle so many things can take place that will cause a disaster I would like call "Ticking Time Bomb." Because in a sense this is a bomb waiting to explode, emotions are a very serious ordeal when it comes to relationships and dating. It sometimes can get even more serious with age as well. How so you ask? Let's look at the entertainment industry and celebrities or even everyday people. This 2-wheel motion cycle and my philosophies are proven constantly over and over again. Example: Let's look at couple that has done well for themselves and has created a lifestyle that only you and I can imagine. He or She has been with each other even before the lifestyle was created. But afterwards, things start to fade out between the two because of hectic schedules and distractions from the bond that has been built over the years. They separate to gather thoughts on what they want to do *(**They are back at cycle 4 in Chapter 1, Decisions**). But things begin to take a turn because instead of fully closing the bond and emotional cycle that they have with each other, they start bringing others into the fold. Meaning that instead of them deciding what the outcome shall be. Also, them fully replenishing themselves with the emotional bond that they have, others are now brought into this emotional rollercoaster "Instant Consoling." Let's take it even a little bit further, during that Instant Consoling period that they are going through, two months goes by. They're enjoying the time spent, the laughs, the instant consoling or feel good period. But remember, there was no closure or any decisions made on the emotional bond that they have had prior to. As matter of fact the two have not talked or even seen each other. So, they don't know what's been going on for the last 60 days in each other's lives. **(This is why the 2-wheel motion cycle is TRICKY)** One day they're out and about around town, they see each other in some* *random place. Instantly, the two begin to talk and catch up. But something happens; the two individuals realize that they are still in love with each other deeply. But what about the other people that brought into the fold that started falling for them and getting that emotional connection with them as well?*

This is why the "Rebounding Period" and the "2-wheel motion cycle" are so tricky. Because during this time people think and feel that they have given themselves the proper time to heal and break that emotional connection that they have with someone. We all have gone through this sometime in our lives. Personally, I will be the first to say that this process was not easy. If a person truly wants to be happy and understand their worth in dating and relationships, the proper steps should be taken to decipher through what will not waste their time. The simplest things in dating and relationship people take for granted. Also, don't realize that your time is your most valuable asset in life. As stated before many would be denial and would not admit that they have been at fault in participating in this period. But during the "Rebound Period" your time is so precious and it is being wasted at this point. Meaning that what value this adds to your life when you settle and set yourself up to fail in this dating and relationship arena. If every person, man or woman, truly take the time needed after every relationship to simply replenish and emotionally cleanse themselves of that emotional baggage. Then each and every person would have a clear mind frame on how to distinguish great value.

Chapter 3: "30 Minute Love"

"30 Minute Love" is something that people experience every day. But often, this is the part that goes unspoken about from time to time. The "30 Minute Love cycle" is simply something that I use to basically go in more depth detail on the phrase "Microwave men and women." People love the feel of the microwave effect and especially in their love life. People love the feeling of feeling good for the moment or just one of those naïve hopeless romantics' that think every person is prince charming.

Better yet you have men also just simply thinking that this is the one to take home to momma. The microwave effect is simply describing people that are only in your life for a season. People that aren't meant to add any type of value to your life and/or people that are only with you for the benefit of themselves. People in the dating and relationship world settle for what they think is value, but they only cause themselves a lifetime of hurt and pain. Especially, when they fall salve to the microwave effect and not follow the proven guidelines to decipher between what won't waste their time. Granted some people love the microwave effect and some love the fact that a person can make them feel good for a moment. But the thing that begins to happen is that both men and women begin to place themselves in a particular category that is a lifetime habit in dating if not broken. I call this category the "Eternal Seeker." This is something that begins to build inside of a person once they have not set any boundaries for themselves in dating. Also, this comes into place when a person has not set any type of value on themselves for what they deserve. Meaning, that when it comes to dating you have to set boundaries and uphold your values on some things that are in your life.

Most would deny being an Eternal Seeker. But let me ask you this, how would you know? Let's examine and go in more detail on the phrase.

"Eternal Seeker"

There are a lot of people that fall in this category of dating for so many reasons. Dating and relationships are so intense to the point of being out of sync and unbalanced as stated in chapter 1. An eternal seeker can mean so many things when it comes to dating and relationships. But the biggest and most important thing to remember is that this is not a great category to be placed in. Reason being, you become complacent in settling and not having a concrete understanding of what your true worth is. Being placed in this realm of being an eternal seeker you devalue yourself on what you deserve and you continue to fall for what will waste the most valuable asset you have in life, which is TIME.

*People become victim in this category without even realizing it or looking at their actions when they have gotten to the point of not knowing their worth. There are 2 main concise ways to become an eternal seeker, a bad relationship and your childhood. A bad relationship can truly cloud a person's mind on some things. But it can also mess them up mentally and internally as well. Example **(This can go for either man or woman**): Let's look at a couple that has been together or married for quite some time. Secretly the husband was living a double life or whatever the case maybe. The relationship ended on bad terms and the woman was deeply in love with the man, headed over hills as a matter of fact. So mentally she is vulnerable in so many areas. Also, her mental state is not clear on making a sound decision on some things. **(Now here is where it begins)** In her mind she has already determined that she cannot live without him, but internally a seed is planted. She wants to fill that void and the lack of what was missing from what she had once before. So she* *continues to seek out something that could possibly fill that void of emptiness. This can go both ways as well. Men, we go through this eternal seeker stage and don't even realize it. Most would say that it is in our nature to seek out women or sleep with multiple women. But my views and philosophies are a bit deeper when it comes to this. Men go through very emotional relationships as well. We have relationships that play on our minds and cloud our judgment just as much as women. But once we have those one or two bad relationships or dating experiences, something changes inside of us internally. Our brain shifts to hunt mode, which is being an "Eternal Seeker." Once this happens, the spirit of fear has been embedded inside of us when it comes to the emotional state of getting our heartbroken. Because at the end of the day even though we want to experience that blissful happiness when it comes to dating and relationship, at that point we are fearful. Fearful of the unknown with new adventures in this regard, so this is where that seed planted inside of us. Therefore, we equip our mindset to not wanting to experience hurt in that facet ever again. When this happens to anyone, this makes them lose sight of what their value and worth is. That's why cycle 3 in chapter 1 is so vital and evident. The getting over your past hurt phase is so critical under the description of the Eternal Seeker. Reason being, simply once you give yourself time to heal from those past hurts and exfoliate your emotions from those bad seeds and relationships in your life. Your mind will become clearer on what you are worth and you won't devalue yourself on what you deserve.*

An Eternal Seeker describes so many people when it comes to dating and relationship. Your childhood plays a major significant role in dating. It is also one of the main reason people fall into the eternal seeker category. How so do you ask? Men and women reciprocate in their adult years what has been instilled in them during their childhood years from their parents. Those examples have a major impact on dating and relationships in the regard of both sexes. During early childhood, little girls look up to and adore their fathers. During adult years, women are usually attracted to men that have some of the same characteristics of their father. Because at that age he is the only male in her life that truly cultivate her and teach her about men. Then you have some that grow up without that father figure. These are the little girls that begin to seek for something or someone to fill that void in their adult years. Sometimes even out through their whole life. Now granted, you have some women that are more impacted be their mothers in their childhood for two reasons. First, some are raised in single parent homes without that male role or figure being present. Secondly, the mother showcases several men around the daughter and brings them in out of her life. So, in this case the little girl is going to feel that this is ok to do and reciprocate.

Then you have the little boys that are always taught to protect "momma." Growing up momma is always the first woman we encounter.

She is the one that shields us and teach us about how women are. Also, most importantly at that age "momma" teaches us how to treat women. Growing up the characteristics and traits that our mother had are some of the same traits that we look for in our women. Sometimes this can also put a strain on us dating and having successful relationships. Because certain people, media, and women would probably consider this being a momma's boy. This is true to a certain extent. But retrospect there is so much more significance behind that analogy that supersedes the momma boy theory. Looking at how a man treats his mother is an encryption of how a man will treat his girlfriend or wife. Meaning that starting out from an early age a man is thought how to treat women by his mother. She was being the example of that in his life growing up. Also, her being a life test drive and teacher on these teachings of how to treat a woman. Now for the manhood part, this is where the father and male figure comes into play. This can work synergistically with the teachings of the mother on how to treat a woman. However, this can also mix like oil and water with the male figure or father being the picture. Manhood as a child is exerted from the fathers or male figures in our lives, whether it's positive or negative. As boys, we tend to gravitate towards the actions of the male figure in our lives. We want to do everything like him or just even looking for that male bonding, support, and love. I guess you could say more so of a hero in a sense. But mainly this is where our manhood is instilled in us, coming from the male roles in our lives. This can be a very detrimental component in the dating and relationships, more or less, this can be the icing on the cake for us as well. At this point early on, we go through this period of trying to find ourselves. This period is typically starts at the age of 6, some boys may start later on. But this is where we are so in tune with everything around us and we try to mimic. When I say try to find ourselves, meaning that whatever male role or figure we have in our lives during this time we will try to mimic everything that this person does.

Whether it's positive or negative during this time we yearn for that approval from our male figures or father. This usually last all the way up until late in the teen years. Now let's go in more detail about this phase to prove my point or philosophies. Between the ages of 6-16 are critical points of manhood teachings for young boys. Mothers can only teach young boys so much on being a man but they can counter act the teachings as well from the male figures. Meaning that if the young boy encounters a situation between the mom and dad or male figure, seeing the man being abusive, violent, and belligerent on so many levels; even though in his mind he wants to protect momma he is also wondering "is this how I am supposing be when I get older." At that point on, there are seeds planted in the young boy's mind on how to be a man. Also, seeing that, he begins to correlate if this is how a man is supposed to treat a woman. Young boys reciprocate any actions that are being shown or seen at that age. That's why in adult years you have so many men that pay respects to "momma" and very few that pay respects to their "fathers".

The "Eternal Seeker" phase is so critical and very profound in a person life. Therefore, essentially describes whole-heartedly the way a person is mentally when walls are built. People in life deny their past hurts and try to run away from the fact of things that has happened in their past. Negating that this is the reason they are the way they are. Then as a result, can't seem to have a successful relationship or dating experience. "30 Minute Love" is an encryption of how the 21st century of dating and relationships are. As stated before out through this chapter, people love that gratification of feeling good for the moment and the right now feeling. Your value should be much higher than an instant gratification. Then the most common that falls into this category of dating, are the ones that on the outside seem to have high values and standards for what they are worth. But that smoke screen comes down and they begin to show that their worth means nothing when they continue that constant cycle of "30 Minute Love." Even myself, I have been at the forefront of this analogy many times before. There was a point in my life where I knew what I was worth and could offer, but my actions shown otherwise. I can truly attest to this theory and concept of the "30 Minute Love cycle" and also being an "Eternal Seeker." It wasn't until I came to grips with myself and took time to understand why I was the way I was mentally. I had to face my past hurts, depressions, and let downs in relationships head on before I could truly have the dating experience and relationship that I wanted. I began to decipher between what won't waste my time and what will. Now granted, I am not saying that every dating experience or relationship is going to be perfect. But what I am saying is that once you take the time that you need to truly understand why you are the way you are mentally on something's. Then face your past hurts and follow the steps of observation and evaluation in dating and relationships. You will come to grips with what your worth really is and be able to decipher between the BULL with a clear distinct mind.

Chapter 4: Mind over Matter

Have you ever heard of the phrase, "Mind over Matter"? Well this can also apply to the meaning of what a relationship is all about, a successful one that is; but the thing that tends to happen is that people have the tendency to get involved in things that they are truly not ready to bare. Meaning that people let emotions and others control their love life and relations in this regard; because the world and individuals that are closest to you have the most uncontrollable influence on some of the decision that you make in life and in your love life. Truly harnessing your worth and understanding what your value is not only in life but also in dating and relationships, is the essence to the whole mind over matter theory in dating. I call this theory "Kryptonite".

Individuals would not believe that this simple theory or this metaphoric analogy goes much deeper than what the text book meaning of the phrase truly is; I apply this to the essence of dating and individuals' personal development. Let's go deeper in this theory in much greater detail:

Kryptonite

Just like in the movie "Superman", his weakness was not that of this earth or anything that a mere human could do; but it was a crystal called kryptonite. Every time a villain would have this object in their possession, they would have him weak to the point of them being able to cause harm for that short period. See, this is how this can apply to your relationship and your self-worth; meaning that people that you have in your life wasting one of the most valuable asset that you have in your life, which is time, that person could be considered your "kryptonite". Meaning that in your relationship, marriage, or even dating if you are with someone that does not uplift you, add to you, empower you, and make you better in every aspect of your life spiritually, mentally, physically, and emotionally then this person is draining life from you instead of adding life to you. The area where individuals make this common mistake is when they move on from relationship to relationship carrying on that same baggage from previous relationships and not giving themselves the proper time to heal from the drainage that they experience from the "Kryptonite" of their past. Not giving ourselves that proper time to heal, we fall subject to that weakness or kryptonite every time it resurfaces in our lives; causing conflict and strains on your present and what could be potentially be our God's Gift.

If what I am saying has not registered yet and has not helped you to understand your worth to a certain degree, this example will. There was a young woman that was three months away from graduating from college with the ambitions of being an actress and a model; she would have one on one practice sessions with her drama instructor while in college, play auditions, and over the summer breaks she would continue to perfect her craft. While getting prepared for a major practice session for the end of the school year play, she met someone that caught her attention, instantly she was moved by his presence and it was love at first sight. But, she was still in transition from moving passed the issues that she experienced from her previous relationship 12 months ago, but she could not have helped the way she felt. She experienced so much abuse and verbal abuse that it broke her down to her lowest point in life. Now here is where everything starts to happen. Instead of her going with her first mind and just staying focused on her acting and major play that she has coming up, she decides to go against her gut feeling and pursue interest in the young man. They hit it off very well, she felt as though he compliments her mentally, spiritually, physically, and emotionally; so, she thought. At this point, both men and women, tend to lose themselves before getting to their deepest root and core of life's greatest project. Remember in my first book "The Power Within, A Woman's Worth: From Both Sexes" I revealed to you that men have the ability to know when a woman is vulnerable, just from the conversation and interactions that they encounter.

In addition, a person will truly show you who they are after about 65 days; so, during this time the young woman is on cloud nine with her feelings and the way her supposedly newfound love is going. She is so wrapped up in this man, that she loses sight of her own ambitions and career moves. Even though she is on cloud nine with this man, she has already experienced physical, mental, and verbal abuse from him as well; her self-esteem is lower, her drive is gone, and she feels that it is no hope for her in finding something better so she settles. However, in her mind, she is just looking pass the issues of her relationship for the sake of saying that she has a good man. On the night before the year ending screen play that could possibly be the beginning of her acting and modeling career or stop it where it lies, which is in college; the two got into a very heated argument over her seeing him with another woman. She was to the breaking point with all the cheating and the abuse that she tells him that it is over and she never wants to see him again. See instead of her truly getting to the root of his issues and hers, using the observation of evaluation method; she went into this situation head first based on emotion and feelings; not knowing that he has rejection and separation issues that stemmed from his childhood that causes him to lash out violently. The night before the play which could have been the start of her career in acting and modeling, this would be her last night on earth. While the young man was dealing with his own issues and his triggers, he brutally beat the young woman to death; saying these words while brutalizing the young woman, "If I can't have you then no one can have you."

So, at this point you should be thinking to yourself, "What is my kryptonite in my life and my relationship?" I bet you are saying to yourself that this could not and would never happen to me, but just think about all the women and men that have made this statement before, but therefore never had the opportunity to retract this statement because it was too late. Individuals never take the time to stop to think about the mind over matter theory when it pertains to dating. In my opinion, the reason being is that we as individuals want to have that peace of mind of being with someone so bad, that we sometimes forget that there are certain principles and guidelines that we must follow when wanting a successful relationship. Just like in business there are keys to being successful, there are keys to have a successful relationship or dating experience. Most would say that it is not that serious when it comes to dating and finding love, but, understand this as stated before when it comes to dating and finding love you will not be taken serious unless you take yourself serious in this area of your life. Through my experience, analogies, philosophies, and advice on helping individuals in their relationships I drew up five principles of having a successful relationship, which I call "5 Laws of Harnessing your Worth".

5 Laws of Harnessing Your Worth

As stated before, dating can be looked upon as a business or you are starting a new venture. In business, everyone wants to be successful and acquire the fruits from their labor in working to achieve success; but, understand that there are keys to becoming successful and being in that position of wealth. This is how individuals should look at dating or their love life; it is the same way in retrospect. Many people don't see or understand it because they never take the time to grasp this concept, so they just dive head first into the shark's mouth and try to learn as situations happen; without getting to the deep core issue of what is really going on. Harnessing your worth is broken down into five laws to guide a person to understand their value and know that they are worth much more than their passed kryptonite's that they have been experiencing. Let's take a deeper observation in these "5 Laws".

Law 1: "Get to your Deepest Root"

Everyone is looking for love and wanting to have the one person that is truly their God's Gift, but, the most common mistake that people make is that they go about doing it wrong; trying to reinvent the wheel or skip steps along the way. We tend to carry our pain and hurts from previous relationships on to the next relationship and to the next; not giving ourselves time to heal and be restored fully from those hurts. Mostly, both men and women don't understand why they are the way they are mentally and emotionally when it comes to dating. Often, the reason being is because we don't look at ourselves and get to the deepest core root of our issues when it comes to dating; which sends us in a constant cycle of hurt, deception, and pain. It's like you're on a rollercoaster ride with your love life and you will continue to ask yourself the same questions of "Why".

When individuals are tired of being sick and tired, going through the same thing, and being on this continuous spiral of constant hurt, often, that's when both men and women will come to grips with themselves and get to the deepest root of their life's greatest project which are themselves. If you are truly looking to find love, you first must be in a position to receive it. Meaning that if you are still dealing with the kryptonite's of your past and all the emotions that comes with it, how can you make room for your

God's Gift that is meant to pour life into you and not take life from you. To understand this and get to that point, you have to come to grips with reality and get to the deepest root of your core issues in life.

Law 2: "Ownership"

After coming to grips with yourself and getting to the deepest core root of your life's greatest project, you must now take ownership of your issues and not run from them. The thing that I find that most individual's do that not only stagnates them in relationships but also in personal development, is that we tend to negate what the real issue is and choose not to face it. In doing this, this can create a multitude of ongoing issues to resurface in your life because you have not faced your triggers that keeps you in bondage mentally and emotionally.

The reason that we try to negate our deep core issues, is simply because we care what people think of us and there is a fear embedded deep within us on knowing who the real us is, which stagnates our growth as a person, which also can have a huge mental and emotional impact on us when it comes to dating. To truly understand and love someone else, we must free ourselves of the emotional weight that we carry around with us from every relationship that we have had and then take ownership of those issues. Meaning, that you cannot let your past dictate your future and keep pushing you away from your God's Gift in life; because doing this you are only crippling yourself.

Law 3: "Self-Reflection"

This is the point where things get very difficult for you in your personal development and when trying to harness your worth, because after taking ownership of your core issues in life that stagnates you from being prepared to receive your God's Gift; you begin to self-reflect on what you are taking ownership of. Meaning that this is where you're looking at the person in the mirror and coming face to face with everything and the issues you have. What people must understand is that in dating and having a successful relationship, you cannot reinvent the wheel and negate the proven steps to understanding your value. I truly can attest to this law being very difficult, because it was very difficult for me. The hardest thing in the world is for a person to come face to face with their past issues and really try to deal with them head on. Reason being is because we're afraid of ourselves in this regard, that's why we go from relationship to relationship with baggage thinking that something new can cover up the damage of what our past must bring.

When I was at this point, coming to grips with me and trying to figure out why then were all my relationship ending the exact same way; it was because I have not gotten to the core root of my issues with my childhood and the fact I was at some point a womanizer later on looking for love, basically denying the fact of what I was or had become. See, I wanted love, needed love, and was ready for that companionship of my God's Gift but my actions showed and demonstrated something totally different; which pushed me further and further away from the one that was specially made for me. Self-reflecting in my opinion is the most complicated law to grasp and was most certainly the most difficult for myself, reason being also, is because when you are trying to reshape yourself and your inner-self people always remind you of how you use to be and what you use to do. This alone can hinder your self-reflecting process if you let it.

At this point, people that you thought that were for you and had your best interest at heart are the very same people that will not take heed to your change or reshaping. Most of them but not all will be the very people that remind you constantly of what you use to do and what you use to be; constantly living in the past and becoming your kryptonite in your life. When you are in the mind set of wanting change in your love life and personal life development, you must treat it as a new construction site. Meaning, that when your mind shifts to the point of operating in the new, you can't build on top of the old simply because of those deep buried spiritual roots that you are constantly piling baggage on; you are still giving your old access to your new operations. In most cases, often, this is where most people get stuck in this process; because we as individuals like to take the easy way out in a lot things. Henceforth, using others to mask the things that we have not dealt with and continuing to cripple ourselves from our true essence.

Law 4: "Healing Time"

This law is where individuals try to reinvent the wheel, when this is the very law that should never be skipped by no means. This is devoted time that should strictly be about you and your growth; getting to that point in your life where you are seriously tired of the constant cycle and rollercoaster whirl winds of your love life going downhill. Taking this time to concentrate on your growth and development of self, diverting that energy of hurt and deceit to something much more meaningful can truly show a person how strong they are and you can harness your true potential in certain areas. Through this time individuals can truly harness their inner gifts and a power deep within themselves when they divert that energy during this healing period, but, most never see it that way because they are concerned with the instant gratifications of being loved or shown affection by the opposite sex to try to bury those deep-rooted issues that they have or had.

Healing time is meant for just what it says, heal. Not meaning spend all your days crying and gossiping to your close ones about how bad this individual has hurt you or how wrong they were for what they have done. You give a person too much power over you when they are constantly dominating your thought process in that fashion. The healing time process is a process where you can truly come to grips with who you are, whose you are, and what you are when comes to this thing we call "Life" and you can truly tap into your subconscious mindset. You regaining the power of your emotions and beginning to dominate your thoughts of what matters the most in this process, which is you. This is the reason why after you have cried and shed your tears you must dig deep and gather all the negative energy and divert it into something positive; regaining your power within and harnessing your worth.

Law 5: "Replenish"

After dealing with all the emotions that will arise from the previous four laws, you come to the stage where everything begins to become clear and you are fully in tuned with your inner-self; knowing who you are, whose you are, and what you are. You are, "Replenished"; replenished from every emotional and mental barrier that has stagnated you in life and in your love life, you have now gotten to the point of truly knowing who you are and no one can come to tell you differently nor deter you away from knowing this. Understanding the previous four laws and getting to this point of operating in law five takes a great of discipline and patience, because of the kryptonite's of your past will resurface and you coming face to face with the one thing that you fear most; which is you. Coming face to face with that fear of truly dealing with our deepest core issues blocks us from progressing and hinders us from receiving our God's Gift in relationships.

When you become replenished, you are cleansed internally so that it can show externally. Understanding and knowing your worth in dating you must take the time to do the work on yourself first, not negating any steps, and understand the importance of these five laws; once this is achieved, you will not allow anyone to come into your love life or love space that is less then what you deserve. You will then be able to decipher between great value and/or life consumers with clear emotional mind and judgment.

Case Study #1:

Rebounding, a situation that I am sure mostly everyone can relate to; this is a situation that has consumed me before I learned how to deal with pain and hurt. In my professional opinion, I feel that we are literally afraid to deal with our truths and hurts when it comes to relationships; because of what we may find out about ourselves. I have advised hundreds of singles and couples over the years, surprisingly one of the biggest outcomes that I come across are both men and women stating that they are not over their previous relationship and it comes out that they have been using someone else to mask their hurt of separation. A few years ago, there were two couples that I was coaching in their relationship and helping them deal with the issues that they had going on. (Due to a confidentiality clause, I will refer to each couple as Couple 1 and Couple 2.) Both couples had a multitude of things going on that caused a disconnect, discomfort, and loss of the emotional connection between the two. **Couple 1:** Awesome couple, on the outside looking in they would appear to have everything that you would literally want in a relationship. They appeared to have great conversation, a great emotional connection, and the love that every relationship would typically desired. However, behind closed doors they were emotionally staving and dying; they were killing each other's spiritual and subconscious being. Meaning, that when you are in a relationship with someone and a piece of you is out of sync from that relationship then you are depriving that person and yourself of growth internally or possibly even the growth that they need to go to the next level themselves in that season of their lives.

Each person in this relationship had dark secrets and feelings that they were keeping from each other, not secrets pertaining to their relationship but secrets of the real reason why both were holding back from giving the full percentage needed for growth in that relationship. In the ten sessions that we had, it was revealed that each person was not over their past relationship fully. Each person has been having secret phone conversations and meet ups with that person from their past, which therefore, caused a deeper more emotional disconnection and discomfort between the two. With the man, this was the same woman that each of his friends and family have warned him about. Prior to getting involved with his now fiancée, his ex-left him broken, abused, and bankrupt; he knew without a shadow of doubt that she was not the woman that was meant to be his God's Gift in life, but it was something about his past that he could not shake or get over. (*Right here at this very moment proves my theory, the universe has a way of testing us when feel that we gotten over our past hurts and emotional scars.*) Although, they never connected on a physical level while he is currently with his fiancée; the emotional and mental cheating is that much greater than the physical. However, his girlfriend on the other hand was a little bit different; she was consumed by the physical nature of her ex and the way he satisfied her intimate needs. See, in this situation the roles were reversed, she did not feel intimately connected with the current man in her life and use to always think about how her past made her body feel. Reluctantly at first, she turned down the advances made by ex to want to meet up but lunch but she would cave into the temptation of just seeing him. On occasions, they would have secret and random meet ups that went from maybe once a week to about 3 or 4 times a week during lunch hours at work. The physical nature between the two was so strong that her physical feelings lead her to fall back in love with her past and vice versa with her current boyfriend as well, in all the meet ups and phone conversations he has admitted to falling back in love with his past and as well his now fiancée admitting to the same. Most would ask the question, "Why won't they just call of the engagement and get back with their past?" That would be true, but we must take a serious hard look at why did that person become a part of our past in the first place. Oftentimes, I find that when there is a lack in a specific area in our relationship; instead of effectively communicating that lack with our partner our minds subconsciously go to a point of seeking out on how to fill that void of lack.

Meaning, even though sometimes we may not go through the actual physicality of fulfilling that lack, but, we will do a play by play in our minds with the person that we would want to fill that lack for us; which in turn somehow will attract that person into our lives. This is how we sabotage ourselves from being truly happy all the way across the board; we fall victim to the instant and right now feelings oppose to what is meant for us long term. **Couple 2:** This situation was a bit different. In this one relationship, both seem head over heels for each other. Every time you see them, it was like a new-found puppy love type chemistry going on, even after 6-years of being together as boyfriend/girlfriend then and 4-years of being engaged; so collectively they have a total of 10-years being together in each other's lives. So, one would think that this was solid and that this was a strong foundational relationship. *(Let me just say this or give a nugget of advice very* *bluntly, if either man or woman is willing to be engage to someone for 4-years with no date set in mind for the actual nuptials in mind to take place; both of you will continue to be alone or a forever boyfriend/girlfriend. This is what you will continue to attract to yourself into your life throughout the course of your life.)* There were a lot of underlining variables and secrets on both parts they were revealing. This was one of those situations where if one person hurt the other, then the other person had to return the hurt 10-times worse than what was given. This went on for years in this relationship but neither wanted to let the other go. But, instead of talking to each other effectively about the situation at hand and dealing with it head on, they both confided into someone else, which in turn cause more disconnection between the two.

Chapter 5: "*Role of a* MAN"

This is one of the most important parts of dating and relationships, "Role of a Man." As stated before, a woman controls the initial parts of dating but the man is the head of the relationship itself. But in the 21st century of dating this is not the case. In this day and time men have lost touch of being a man and knowing what the "Role of a Man" truly is. Men we have been designed to conquer and be leaders since the beginning of time. But this era has been tainted by so many things and we have fallen short of falling in that role. In dating and relationships now, you have so many women that act as the man and not the woman. Why is that? Let's go in depth of why. The reason why is because men now are not held accountable for not being a man. As a man, we are born with an assignment and a destiny in this life. So, in this world of dating and relationships I use an analogy called "Pussy Footing", to describe the short comings of us as men when we have fallen short of our role and assignment.

"Pussy Footing"

Pussy footing is something that is most commonly used by our parents or grandparents when describing a slothful person. But me, I take it a step further and use that term or phrase to describe us men. In this new era of dating you have men that "Pussy Foot" around their role or calling, especially in relationships and dating. You have men that have women support and provide for them and their well-being, but still expect a woman to submit to them. In dating and relationships, it is our assignment and role to cultivate the woman and uplift her. Not saying, that you should be controlling or domineering. But knowing yourself as a man and a man in Christ would truly give you the understanding of your assignment. Being able to cultivate and replenish a woman's needs on an emotional, mental, spiritual, and intimate level.

Pussy footing around your assignment, role, and responsibilities would not get you the respect you truly deserve from a woman. Simply because it is out of sequence of what it should really be. A lot of men wonder why their women talk to them any kind of way, disrespects them, becomes very deceitful, and etc. The reason is, a woman will only reciprocate the love and affection that you're due based on your leadership. Example: Let's say that you are in a committed relationship and things have been going great for about a few months (At this point you are still in the observation stage of the relationship, women take notes!!!!). *Everything seems to be going well and he appears to have the qualities that you're wanting and need to sustain. That 4th or 5th month comes around and he walks off of his job or gets laid off. You ask him why, he says "Man my supervisor had it out for me and let me go just because!!!" Time goes on and he gets evicted. So, you being the woman that you are, standing by your man say "Babe you can come stay with me until you get back on your feet." Going to pause here and explain a few things. This is why the observation and evaluation period is so evident in today's realm of dating. Because when it comes this new era of dating, you are dealing with a whole new breed of men and women.*

Once you make that statement to a man that says his manager or supervisor just let him go just because; you are setting yourself up for unnecessary drama in your life. How so you ask? Well let's continue with the example. Once he hears those words, some things begin to happen. In your mind, you are thinking that by him being a man and with the ability to work and provide everything will be good for this transition. Not knowing about his work ethic, background, and the core reasons why he is the way the he is. So, he moves in with you, you're excited because you got your man close to you. Also, you're able to have that companionship that you want. You ask him, "So babe how is the job search going and what your plans on something's are?" He says, "It's going, but you know I am just chilling right now, taking everything in and weighing my options." You are being considerate and understanding of his situation you cook, clean, pay for the dates when you two go out, and etc. But you realize something, it has been 9 months and you still find him sitting on the couch most days watching Reality Shows and playing video games, still yet to find a job. This is a true example of Pussy Footing, meaning instead of truly taking advantage of that situation, showing your manhood, and stepping into that role of a man. He became complacent and comfortable with his woman being the breadwinner and staying with her. Situations like this are things that happen every single day and a lot of women are fooled by this in the beginning stages of a relationship.

Men should be held accountable for upholding manhood and being a man. Being a man does not just mean being a provider, but also you have to be the HEAD and know that role. Being able to fully lead, conquer, and being a cultivator in any situation; these characteristics have to exude from us in this regard. Most would misinterpret what I am saying as being controlling, possessive, and domineering. But that's just your way of thinking in this regard. Elevate your mind and understand what your calling and assignment really is as a man. Especially in this dating and relationship world there are some things that we must do on our part. Once a man truly knows himself as a man and a man in Christ he then will know what his true calling is to a woman. Once this happens the flow of the relationship will be that much better. Then you will truly understand and have your relationship desires. There are 3 things that I feel that men should be held accountable for when falling into that Role as a Man in the relationship and dating arena: **_Leadership, Provider, and Cultivator._**

These 3 core things mean so much in falling into that Role as a Man. We as men are called to do so much more than what the world has set forth us to be or has placed in the lime light. Each essential characteristic is so vital to the description of how a man should be especially pertaining to dating and relationships.

Leadership:

Leadership is something that is built inside of us as a man, whether we are exemplifying good or bad leadership characteristic. But in dating and relationships, this is where we get our respect as a man from women. As stated before, a woman's love, affection, and respect is reciprocated based on the leadership of a man. This is an essential tool that women look for in a man in the dating and relationship world. Leadership can mean so many different things: how you command respect but *slow to wrath, how you stand by your faith in God, standing by your morals as well, etc.*

Provider:

Being a provider has been so misconstrued in the 21st century of dating, that it will blow your mind. Under this characteristic trait, there are women superseding the man in this position. The reason this so out of sync with the plan, is simply because that is not the way it was designed nor was that the purpose of what supposed to be. Men are thought to be head, provider, and to protect our families. It is in us and it is a part of our male genetic DNA. Granted, things may happen out through the course of a relationship that may set you back on some things but, as a man this is where your manhood is exemplified. Knowing how to bounce back and assure the woman that it will be ok and that she is secure.

Cultivator:

Cultivation, in my opinion is so very important in this realm of dating and pertaining to us men. You have a lot of men that do not *understand this role or this particular trait that we have. It is very powerful in relationships, and honestly it would make the relationship go that much smoother ****(This only works ladies if the man is truly genuine and wanting something long term)***. Everyone needs a bit of cultivation in their lives, but it is our duty to cultivate our woman and encourage her to the point of total bliss. We as men must take that role speaking positivity over her life, build her up, support her, and enrich her with the abundance of true gentleness and sincerity. Once these traits are eternalized in us and we truly understand what our role is. We can therefore exemplify and fall into our true calling as a man in this realm of dating and relationships.*

Chapter 6: Love vs. In Love

In dating, this is one of the most misconstrued concepts there is; the love or being in love concept. Often, people confuse this as being one in the same, which it is not, it is very different and far from the same. Love or just saying the three words I love you is commonly used in today's time and used most cases in a sense of just getting what you want at that time. Both men and women have used these three words or the phrase of love for a certain motive or gain of some sense; making the person at that time feel good or feel loved to get what they want before a major let down. In the dating game, we all have used these three words at some point in time and knowing that we did not mean it or just saying it because the other person has stated it to us as how they feel about us; we all are guilty of it, be honest. But, without even realizing it, in dating we create stagnation in ourselves when it comes to finding our God's Gift and resentment to the expression of being in love. Meaning, that we have falsified this expression of love or the endearment of love so much that when it truly comes along we won't even recognize it and this constantly pushes us away from being prepared to receive our God's Gift in our love life.

Being in love comes from a deeper place within us, it is not forced and it is not a falsified expression. It is something that comes natural and an expression that connects two spirits in harmony; not saying that everyone that you are in love with will be your God's Gift but what I am saying is the expression of being in love and the act of being in love between two people can be magical, if the proper guidelines are followed. As stated in my first edition book entitled, The Power Within, A Woman's Worth: From Both Sexes, you cannot find true love and prepare for your God's

Gift in dating by skipping steps. There are guidelines and steps that you must follow in finding that person that is solely designed for you. Individuals get so wrapped up in the fact that they are single and don't have anyone right now at this present time, that they forget about what this time is truly meant for. Being single is not meant for you to have a pity party and invite your friends over for a glass of wine and finger foods to share your sob stories on how all of you are single. This is the time and moment in your life *(if you are serious about your love life)* where you can seriously maximize the guidelines in dating and finding love; without skipping either step to get to the next step. Meaning, this is the time that you truly harness your worth and value in this regard; make love to yourself, not literally, but spend that invested intimate time with yourself to become one with yourself; releasing yourself of the emotional baggage that has drained and drew life from you over the years. This is the point where you fall back in love with yourself, so that you can fully be prepared to receive true love once it comes; because if not, as stated before you will build a sigh of resentment within yourself toward love altogether, shunning away from any possibilities of ever feeling this wonderful feeling ever again.

In dating, oftentimes, I find that people are confused with what type of love they are operating in when it comes to what love they are expressing or receiving from another person. Not knowing and understanding love has stagnated a lot of individuals' mind set also from the growth of being able to handle the expression when it appears right in front of them or in their lives; and this occurs for two reasons. First reason, as stated in my first edition book "The Power Within, A Woman's Worth: From Both Sexes", your childhood has a lot to do with how you perceive love as an adult. Not properly seeing the right way to show affection, traumatic verbal/physical abuse, no mentoring, and nurturing to the fact of understanding how love truly operates as a child growing up. Secondly, traumatic heartbreak or falsifying the expression of love can truly blind you from what God is ready to bless you with in your love life. Going through a heartbreak is not meant for you to stay there in that mindset forever and grieve, therefore, the longer you have a pity party on the negativity that has taken place the more it dominates your thoughts and you attract what you think about most, i.e., a person with the same characteristics of the one that broke your heart prior to. As a young man in my early 20's, I was taught about the types of love from a Biblical and Greek standpoint; now that I am an older and a bit wiser I understand and see all five types of love that we as people operate in. Some which can be very detrimental to the progression of us as person and in our relationships, if not handled accordingly. Let's go in more detail about the "5 Types of Love."

5 Types of Love

Mania:

This type of love is expressed by many people in relationships. This type of love is that obsessive and possessive type of love; expressing it in the form of jealousy. So many people let this form of expression pertaining to love dominate their thoughts, minds, and emotions; driving them to operate out of the norm of their character or habits. I personally can attest to fully operating in this expression of love, because at the time I was operating in a form of control and being controlling; being a womanizer and dictator in the fact of instilling fear to receive what I wanted. Not knowing and understanding the damage that I was doing not only to myself but to the mentality of the women I encountered at that time during this period of my life. Operating in this type of love is not only detrimental to you in dating, but it is also very damaging to you long term. Because psychologically and spiritually this expression of love can push you further away from the manifestation of your true gift in dating and relationship. Meaning that operating in this love expression or staying in a situation where it is stagnant based on this love type, you could be potentially letting the one that is meant for you pass you by; which can cause years of your life to go by in unhappiness and not being fulfilled.

Eros:

This form of love is something that so many people can relate to and that is Eros love. Eros is a Greek word derived from the word "erotic", this is that passionate and lustful type of love; no feelings and/or emotions tied to this type of love. So many people fall slave mentally to this form of expression because we operate in lust and in unemotional intimacy. In dating, this love expression can damage everything that we try to accomplish in our love life without us even knowing it. Ask yourself this one question, "After that thrill is gone from casual intimacy (**Eros love expression**), what do I really have that is substantial?" Think about this for a minute, in dating this love expression is what places us in a rebound and satisfy my needs state of mind. Because, as stated before if you do not give yourself the proper time to be freed from all your inner baggage you are just making deposit of counterfeit emotions and feelings; basically, transferring your pain and baggage to the next person through intimacy. Eros love can be a very pleasant expression but only if utilized properly and not for leisure. Once we understand the difference between each expression we are operating in or receiving, only then we can begin to harness our inner potential and reciprocate accordingly.

Phillos:

This love expression is most common among us as individuals; this is that brotherly, family, or friendship type love. This is referring to our best friend, our BFF, or maybe that favorite family member that you grew up with in your childhood years; but guess what, this love expression can potentially cause stagnation in your love life as well. See, to truly harness your worth and understand your value in dating, certain people will not be able to go with you on this journey. Meaning, everyone that say they are for you or have your best interest at heart maybe the hindering factor that is causing you to miss out on upgrading to that next level in your life and love life. Early on in your life certain people may have been right there with you in the beginning encouraging you on, but that is because you were doing the same thing that they were doing or constantly bringing them that same old sob story of your love life. The phillos love expression can be a very tricky expression of love, because in my opinion, with certain people you don't get to see the actual person or the heart of the person until a drastic change occurs in your life.

Storge:

This love expression is another very tricky love expression and sometimes is very hard to draw boundaries around when it comes to dating and looking for love; this love expression is storge. This love is pertaining to the love between parents and their children, the motherly/fatherly love. This love expression can be very detrimental to both men and women in dating and here are two reasons why; Firstly, parents can be so protective over their children to the point of certain qualities and traits not being able to flourish or exude properly. Meaning, a mother or fathers love can be so deep that it can sometimes hinder the natural progressions that need to be established. This is where the term, "Mommy's Boy" or "Daddy's Baby Girl" comes into play. Secondly, much as we don't want our children to experience or go through some of the hurt and pain that we have experienced in our past; subconsciously that is what we are imparting over our child's life. When our fears dominate our thoughts the most that is what we are calling into existence, believe it or not.

Agape:

This love expression is the highest form of love anyone can show; this is that agape love. The example or root of this love expression comes from the love God or Christ have for humankind; the ultimate expression of love, loving someone more than yourself, and putting someone before yourself. I often hear people say that they "love someone more than life itself", but, is that something that we truly mean when we say it. Agape love is that perfect love, loving you passed your pain, fears, flaws, sins, and short-comings; this is the love that God has expressed to us and is still showing us no matter what we do, have done, or have gone through in our lives.

Case Study #2:

In life, we have so many things that we go through that makes up our story. In my life as it pertains to dating and relationships, I have experienced the highs and lows in this area of my life; I chose to expound on myself in detail through this case study as it pertains to this chapter while deeply clarifying my analogy called "4th Quarter Love Theory." Freshmen year of college was the start of everything for me; it was like a world I have never seen before. Having the ability to create whoever I wanted to be in life, I was one of those guys that grew up and did not have a great confidence appeal to women because of me being super shy and reserved; I would always use basketball to release my pain and hurt that I have experience thus far in my young life and to get attention. At that time, I was still battling some deep emotional wounds that I was dealing with that had me confused as a child. However, I looked at this as a way to reinvent myself, being away from home, and away from the spiritual and emotional tension that consumed me mentally; I begun to find myself and my "swag" as the young people would say. During this reinvention of myself women begun to gravitate to me; I portrayed a level confidence like no other and that is what I assumed attracted them to me. During this process, I did not know how to cope with the attention and the affection being shown, so I would accept any and everything that was thrown my way from women no matter if I was talking to someone on an emotional/intimate level or not; not caring about the feelings I was castrating or the pain I was causing. Often, the very things that we do to others, we must receive that back 10-fold.

Therefore, I transferred schools that next semester of my sophomore year and came back home to Memphis; but I was not the same person when I returned. Not caring about school or taking my opportunity for an education at that time was so astonishing it would have blown your mind; I was hurting and did not know it. The way I dealt with my hurt was like drinking a cup full of Lysol; dying inside and emotionally killing myself going from relationship to relationship, woman to woman transfusing my pain onto the next. The level of the emotional baggage and mental baggage I created for myself was so detrimental that I pushed myself seven to almost ten years away from my God's Gift and the path that was meant for my life. During this time, there was not a development of a man but a man that would mask his hurt and fears; I was a womanizer, a dictator, controlling, and said whatever I had to say or do to sleep with whichever woman not knowing and understanding what I was doing to them or myself. When it got to the point where I wanted love and I needed love, I was immensely damaged and broken to the point it was unbearable. I was hurting and the only way that I could release my hurt as stated previously was through sex, transfusing my pain onto women; getting that temporary sigh of relief through pleasure. While going through this downward spiral in dating, I was engaged 3 times and brought 3 rings before I did the work of myself and got to the root of my life's greatest project, which was me. Can you imagine the things that were going on with me mentally to buy 3 rings and have 3 engagements all in a close range of each other, 2 of which being within an 18-month timeframe?

Therefore, during this time I did not follow the proven steps and guidelines to receiving and achieving love in a relationship; successfully that is. As stated previously in chapter 1, we as individuals tend to skip the necessary and vital parts to achieving happiness when it comes to relationships and dating; because we want everything right now and instant. See, this is the very thing that I did to myself; I wanted everything right now in an instant, not thinking about what I had to face down the road of life in this regard. This is where the" 4th Quarter Love Theory "comes into fruition, this works wonders for coming to grips with the issue at hand and I was the issue at that time. The number one of all out of this theory I dealt with greatly was the part where you must "Get Over Your Past Hurts". As I have mentioned before, the universe has a powerful way of testing you and seeing if you are truly ready for what you say you are ready for; or even possibly what you say you are over. You attract into your life what dominates your thoughts the most.

Chapter 7: "Why do Men and Women Cheat"

This must be the most controversial topic pertaining to dating and relationships, period. Especially now in this realm of dating, people still don't understand the reason behind this mishap that has the world assuming and wondering. Well, it took me a great deal of time to actually analyze this question. Most would just flip this and ask, "Why do men cheat." This goes much deeper than a man cheating. This pertains to both men and women in this spectrum of dating and relationships. The world would tell you that the reason a man cheats on woman is because the woman lets him, it is in our nature to be hunters, and have multiple women. This could be true to a certain extent, but me, I see this as something much deeper than that. As stated before it pertains to both men and the women.

The reason that both men and women cheat is simple, in nature and the genetic cycle the man is the head and the woman is submissive to the man. But in this 21st century realm of dating, as stated in Chapter 4, men have fallen short of being true to their calling as a man. So in result of that, we devalue ourselves in sharing our man gift with multiple women. Meaning, that instead of truly honoring what we have been put here in this world for and design to do. We go through what I call "Dumb Man Moments" to learn what our true worth really is as a man. Not saying that you are not expected to make mistakes and go through life lessons in this regard. But what I am saying is that only when a man has it made up in his mind that he is going to truly fall into his role as a man and not be a an "Eternal Seeker." Then at that moment is when he will not cheat and honor his calling. See women are much different, as stated also in

Chapter 4 a woman is taken by a man's *leadership.* Meaning women will only reciprocate the love and affection that you are due based on that quality, your leadership. So, this is the reason why women cheat, it is very hard for a woman to cheat because of the soul ties and emotional connection they have after the fact. But, the reason is that everything results back to the leadership of the man. Meaning, therefore, if that man falls short in his calling or roll as a man the woman does not feel secure nor protected by any means. So therefore, her attention wonders to try to fill that void of what she is lacking. The man is the covering of the woman in dating and relationships. So how can you cover successfully if you have not fallen into your calling fully? I have heard so many reasons and stories pertaining to this that it will blow your mind. If men and women take time to understand the philosophies behind having a successful relationship and knowing that there are things that have to take place in this regard the experience would be endless.

Now granted, understand that everything that I am saying is only pertaining to a person that truly has the mindset and is ready for something long term. Also, truly understanding what their value and worth truly is. This is the true reason why people cheat, men and women, because the order has been broken. Meaning that it all starts with the covering of the woman which is the man, we are the cultivators of women. That's part of what we were designed to do and predestined for. Now, an ordinary person would look at what I am saying and they probably would not see the logic behind this philosophy. But, if people truly understand the order of relationships and dating, understand the things that truly have to take place in order to have a successful one. Even also realize that you have to follow the steps of observation and evaluation. Then people will understand my philosophies and analogies in this spectrum of life. People think that women cheat on the same line as men, this is definitely not the case. Women cheat with their emotions, which is a very hard thing to regain back once she has disconnected herself from you. Simply meaning as stated before it is very hard for a woman to cheat based on this factor. But once they sense or feel that they are neither secure nor protected by any means, women don't cheat right off the bat. But they give you warnings that lead up to that emotional disconnection.

Now you have men and women that have what I call a "Main Player" in their life. This is someone that is considered the person in their life but still they have a backup that caters to a specific need when things go wrong. In dating, most would call this giving yourself options, but me; I call this the *"Sabotage Effect."* The sabotage effect is most common in dating and relationship. People do it without even thinking about how this effect can truly disconnect you from understanding and experiencing the wealth of happiness in this regard.

"Sabotage Effect"

The Sabotage Effect is a very concrete component to why men and women cheat in the 21st century realm of dating. Remember everything that I am saying is pertaining to a person that is truly ready to experience or have something long term and meaningful. People sabotage their own worth and happiness. Meaning that a man or woman can truly have someone that is genuine right in front of them in their life that adds value to them, but they would be distracted by the 20% of what is sent to take them off course.

In this regard, you both have continued to place yourselves in the eternal seeker category in life by constantly playing and devaluing your worth in so many areas. How so you ask? Well, let go in depth. You have a man and woman that have been dating for about 6 months. Everything is going great initially. Both feel that they have found what they have been searching for and things begin to get serious. You both have had some trying times in your life pertaining to dating and relationships. But as you go on you have a few people that are not so convinced by your love and attraction for one another. You have people you know that say to you, "You know how the last one was girl, you need to watch him; he seems sneaky!" or guys, "Man, you need to get you a side piece, just in case this one starts tripping!" Once you have received this those seeds are planted inside of you and you instantly "Sabotaged" your happiness. The sabotage effect does not start externally but internally first. So, as a result of taking in those words and not stopping them in their tracks initially, your mind begins to wonder. Then you find yourself falling for the distractions of the 20%. Because before the point of them saying anything, your mindset was in total bliss and focused on being happy. But after the seeds were planted you also have begun to search for things that were not there. So that opened the door for you to wonder outside that bond you two had.

The Sabotage Effect is as evident amongst us as men, that the results would astonish you. If you would ask 100 men, "How many times they have messed up on relationships that added so much value and positivity to their life?" The answers would blow your mind. I am truly a recipient of this survey; because I have truly been everything that I have stated thus far and have gone through a plethora of let downs in this regard. Even though experiencing those hurts and pains, I have also been the one that caused a plethora of hurt as well. Also, I have observed so many situations that have taken place in my life thus far in different settings. All of those situations have proven every analogy and philosophy that I have stated thus far as well. Once I took the time to restore myself and replenish my internal self. My mind begun to shift to me falling into my role as a man and knowing what my true worth is as a man. At that point, that's when things begun to change externally in my life in this world of dating.

Chapter 8: "Influences, 3 Strands"

As you may know, things are not what they seem to be and the people closest to you really don't have your best interest at heart. So, pertaining to dating and relationships, people look to others for validation on their relationships. Going on to say that influences are a very detrimental component to the whole realm of dating and relationships. Outside influences and the influences of the media has a major impact on how the 21st century realm of dating really is. People misconstrue the elements of dating and having successful relationships. They feel that everyone closest to them knows what's best and what they feel they need. But in reality, the very people that are influencing you to go the other way in your relationship; even tell you that he or she is not for you. These are the same people with shadows and skeletons in their closet as well.

What individuals have to understand is that having a great dating experience and a successful relationship is not done involving other people into the mix. Neither looking out of your eye gates at how others and friend's relationships are taking place. Also, people have to understand and know that there are necessary things that have to take place in order to have the meaningful relationship and dating experience that you want. There was an analogy that was used in a sermon that I once heard from a very prestigious minister from Dallas when I was 21 years old. He stated that in your relationship and marriage, it should be only made up of 3 coils. At that age and time in my life as a young man, his analogy was so profound to me that it stuck with me for quite some time.

But instead of saying 3 coils, I use the analogy of 3 strands. This truly breaks down the philosophy of how dating and relationships should be. Also, how the order of how dating and relationships was meant to be. The media has misconstrued dating and the roles of a relationship so much that the minds of individuals are so out of sync with how it really should be. Now granted, there are people that you may go to for advice in this regard. But it should be just that and nothing more. The close individuals that people go to for relationship advice are the very people that deep down inside would want you to be unhappy or stay in the relationship that is truly not meant for you in your life. The analogy 3 Strands is such an epic description of how the order should be in relationships. ***God the Father (which is the covering of it all), The Man (which is the head of the relationship), and The Woman (which is the intercessor for the man).***

"3 Strands"

As stated before, this analogy is the perfect inclination of how the order of dating and relationships should be. The media, people, and other outside forces has tainted what was really meant to be a joyous experience and most importantly, a happy moment for one's life. Finding love and finding a person that is worth your time, the most valuable asset you have. For example: Let's say you are with someone and you two hit the 2yr mark but have yet to be married. You both have done things in the relationship to cause confusion. But you both are still holding on to that foundation that was built in the beginning. Such as the love you two share and the precious moments that are always cherished memories. **(Here is where it starts to happen typically)** *The communication between the two of you is starting to fade. You both have some concerns that you two want to address, but neither of you want to cause any more confusion. So, you both result to consulting with close friends or some family. Getting their opinion on really what you should be talking to each other about. As you're talking to some of your close friends and some family about* *the situation at hand, some things come into play and begin to happen. That very person that you're talking to that you thought was all for the relationship that you two are in. That person begins to really show you through their opinions how they really feel. Going to pause here for a moment, see at this point of your relationship you have begun to open up doors of destruction in your relationship. As soon as you go from telling a person how well your relationship is to tell them about everything that is going bad in it. At that moment will then get the truth about how that person views you and your relationship. How so you ask?*

Well just think about the last time you were in what you thought was a great relationship. Think about how excited you were. Think about how elated you were to share your happiness with a close friend. Then as time progressed on, you started to experience hardships in that relationship just like everyone else. Needing to vent, you start to share the bad in the relationship with a close friend. These are some of the words that will flow from their mouth, "Girl I told he was no good, he just like every other man!!!" or "You don't need him, you can do badly by yourself!!!" Men, does this sound familiar, "Man I told you she was a gold-digger!" or "Man, if I was you I would go ahead and get me a chick on the side, just in case!"

These things are typically the responses that we get when we consult with outside influences. Then after your consultation, you try to make a rational decision. But your decision is not yours because it's based on the consultation of others. At this point, your 3 Strands are simply made up of something else; the Man, the Woman, and close friends or family. But people really don't understand the simplicity of this analogy. If you would consult with God the Father which in the order of how things should be, is the covering of it all. You would have the sustainable mindset and understanding that you need to withstand any trying time in a relationship.

Chapter 9: Law of Attraction

Our mind is by far one of the most powerful organisms that operate and functions in the human body; but also it can create our reality as well. Our thoughts and the fibers of our mind control how we design our life; our thought process controls what comes in and out of our lives. Most would read this and ask the question of, "How does this pertain to dating and having a successful relationship?" or one would turn and look the other way at this concept of the Law of Attraction in dating and having a successful relationship. But, we have to realize that whatever dominates our thoughts the most will become our reality. If you harbor onto those past feelings and deep emotional wounds of being hurt and being verbally abused years ago, that very thing that dominates your thoughts the most will continue to become your reality in dating; but each time it will be dressed up differently than the last, making it that much harder to detoxify your mind and your emotional wounds.

The Law of Attraction in dating and relationships is what subconsciously makes up the whole dating process of attraction. Here is the reason why, when we first entered the dating world with our very first date as a teenager, that first he/she we dated subconsciously set up our Law of Attraction in dating. Meaning, when we had our very first date and experienced our very first heartbreak, we never forgot it. It has been embedded in our subconscious thinking and emotional consciousness, therefore, since we have never forgotten that first heartbreak we have set the tone subconsciously in our dating life without even knowing it. Each phase or each heartbreak is the same as that first heartbreak, but the difference is that each time it is dressed up differently than the last making it harder to break through those barriers of deceit and that emotional bondage follows behind. So, when you truly get to the core root of the baggage that has entrapped you internally you will find that you are not only dealing with your current emotional baggage in your adulthood but the emotional baggage that has been planted inside you from the start of your whole dating process. Therefore, during this process of dealing with past emotions that has not been released we try to mask our hurt; giving people a false representation of ourselves, which causes us to skip crucial steps in finding love. As I have stated before in my first book entitled, "The Power Within, A Woman's Worth: From Both Sexes" there are guidelines and proper steps that need to take place before you can successfully achieve happiness in your love life; steps in which we are scared to face and we as individuals portray that we don't have time for. But, if we don't have time to really do the necessary work on ourselves and get to the core root of our life's greatest project; then how can we change the course of our past universe in dating from being our current and future universe in our love life?

If you are not ready to do the necessary homework on yourself, change the course of what you attract into your subconscious, and deal with the naked you; then you will forever "Date your Past". See a lot of people missed this concept in the whole dating and relationship process. I am very transparent with my story and the things that I have gone through, this is the one thing that I can truly come to grips with and that is for years before getting married two years ago, I have been dating my past. Dating my Past, what is that some may ask? Let's go in much greater detail on the Dating my Past Theory.

Dating My Past

Most would look at this theory and ask how can this even possibly be a theory or maybe even think of this as being in and out of relationships with a people several different times over the years. But, that doesn't even come close to what this theory actually means or even describe. Ask yourself this question, "How many times have I dated someone and they remained you of what you just left?" See, the dating my past theory, it is a clear and plain breakdown of the Law of Attraction in dating. There was a young man that was very ambitious, outgoing, and very outspoken; one would look at him and say that he is an elite catch on the outside. But, deep inside he had some emotional wounds and scares that was internally killing him; putting his emotional and mental state with love on life support.

But, the only way that he knew that he could mask his pain and emotional emptiness was to transfuse pain and revert back to his old habits. Men, we transfuse pain through sex; so with this young man, this was the only way that he could temporarily deal with his emotional pain and emotional emptiness. Every time it got to a point of remotely seeming like an emotional and committed connection was about to form between him and whoever; he would literally push himself away from the situation. Going to pause right here on this analogy for a minute; see, this is the very thing that both men and women go through but neither take the time or have the courage to actually face that inner pain. We never try to get to end resolve of the hurt or pain that we have buried down inside of us; we use other people to mask our hurt, we use other people and their emotions for that quick fix of a temporary relief of our own bull.

We go through life wondering when will our time come for our God's Gift in dating or even to the same degree, wondering does this person that I am spending my time with reminds me of the last few people that I have dated. Now, back to the analogy; as the young man tried to figure out ways to cope with his buried issues, he realized that working out at the gym was not working for him at all anymore, talking about it to his close colleagues was not working for him anymore, and being alone was not working either. However, him going through the up and down emotions of being taunted by his passed issues, releasing and transfusing that pain through sex was like a fiend looking for that next fix to get him through. Years went by, and the young man came across someone that actually captured his attention as far as him thinking about long term; he begun to evaluate the differences in what he has dealt with in the past and how this one here seems to be the one to make him change his ways. More or less, thinking that she may be the one to take his mind off all of the pain he has caused and all of the pain from his past. This very analogy is the clear depiction of how both men and women view and deal with their past in dating and getting over relationships; instead of us taking the time to be alone and stand in the hurt of our past, we view and see others as being the cure for pain or dealing with our emptiness. Furthermore, we fail to realize the hell that we cause ourselves in doing this; also think about it in this instance, let's just say that this particular person is the one that is truly meant for the young man in this analogy and they met up and etc. By him not being mentally and emotionally prepared to receive what she has to offer him fully, he places himself in what I call an "Emotional Limbo"; meaning, that we place ourselves in a position for something that is meant for us to receive but we are not mentally and emotionally prepared to handle that particular season of our lives at that time.

Therefore, which causes us to be pushed further and further and further away from our creator's manifestation in our lives; hindering us from reaching our full potential in harnessing our worth in this regard. We have to understand how the Law of Attraction in dating plays a major role in our lives when it comes to dating and what we attract into our lives. What dominates our thoughts the most is what we attract into our lives; when we to mask the hurt of our past, we do not get rid of the hurt we only attract more hurt. That is the power of our thoughts in our subconscious, you can literally produce forth the relationship that you want based of what you can attract into your life; but the key is being able to release yourselves of that emotional emptiness and pain that we have buried, not run from it but deal with it. Because it is only going to follow you or come back around full circle ten times worse and hit you head on like a Mack Truck on I-24 going 60mph.

Chapter 10: "God's Gift"

Often time's people pray for God's gift in so many areas of their lives. Even myself, I have prayed for God's gifts pertaining dating and relationships. Having a great relationship and great dating experience in my opinion is done in order and by guidelines. Meaning, that there are certain things that has to take place in order for you to understand, know, and decipher away from the BULL. You have some people that would look at what I am saying and say that these things or my philosophies doesn't work within everyone in this area. I will prove to you in this chapter, if you have not realized any of them by now.

Being able to spend your time with someone that values it and cherish you as a person is God's gift. Someone that connects with you on every level that you need to sustain and maintain in a successful relationship or maybe even dating that will lead to that serious commitment of a relationship. But first, there are some things that have to take place before you receive God's Gift in that area of your life. As stated in chapter 1, you really have to observe the people that you feel mean you some good in that area of your life. For both men and women, only and if only you are truly ready for something serious and long term will my philosophies and analogies hit home with you. A lot of people generally put their emotions and feelings into a person before really understanding and knowing that person. Here is what I mean by that, let's say that a woman is still grieving over a 3 year break up. After that break, she found out that the person she has spent the last 3 years of her life with had another woman on the side and she is expecting their first child. She consults with her close friend over a glass of wine at one of their favorite night spot just to get out. Wanting to free her mind of the situation and just relax. Her and her close friend are sitting their enjoying themselves and then all of sudden they are approached by 2 men. Instantly, there is some level attraction that is between the two. The conversation is flowing pretty well initially so they exchange contact information and part ways. Now, the next day she talks to her friend about the guy that she gave her number to on the previous night. Her friend gives her opinion and tells her that it has been 6 months; you need to start back dating or take applications and have fun. Her friend continues to say, "that you don't need to let your past relationship consume your actions so much."

Now, granted her friend is giving some great advice to a certain extent. But there are 2 things wrong with the situation of her jumping back out on the dating scene. One, she has not fully replenished herself of her emotional baggage. So, her mind and decision making is not clear. Secondly, she is vulnerable to everything that has taken place resulting from her past relationship. In her mind, she is ready to move on but her heart says otherwise. Let's continue with the scenario, she listens to her friend and take her advice. So, she responds to a message of possibly meeting later that week with the guy. She knows in her mind that she is not ready mentally for this. But, she has adopted that mindset of using another person to get over her past, which is a detrimental thing to do. She meets with him at a coffee shop of some sort. Instantly she is attracted to his well-groomed appearance. The conversation starts out with general basic information about the two and then it gets into deeper questions and information as well. **(Women, if you have not taken heed to anything I have stated in this book thus far, take heed to this!!!)** One thing that every man has that I feel that women generally don't pick up on is that every man has the ability to know when a woman is vulnerable when talking with her. This is something that as a man, we can choose to play off of your vulnerability or be there to cultivate you and console you. Well, in this case the man chose to play off of her vulnerability.

As time progress on, the guy already has it made up in his mind that this is going to be an easy task. He begins to feed her things that she wants to hear and tell her that she is different than most of the women he has dated in his life. A few months goes by she feels that God has answered her prayers on sending her someone that is in tune with her emotions and just her as a person. So she begins to be intimate with him over and over and over again. Now in her mind she is over her past and has moved on with her life with someone that she feels is her, "God's Gift." **(Now here is why the initial steps of observation should have fallen in place)** She notices that after 6 months' things have begun to take a 360 degree turn. She notices he has the same characteristics and traits as her past relationship from about a year prior. Then she finds out that she is expecting their first child together as well. But, also what she finds out and realize is that he has a past as well that she did not know about. That he is married with 2 kids already.

Now, this situation proves so much. Because what we think and feel is our "God's Gift" in this world of relationships and dating is very well a distraction that keeps us far away from his true gift for us in that spectrum of our lives. This proves why observations are a very important component to us finding or having that person that is truly "God's Gift." We truly have to give ourselves time to replenish our mind, body, and soul from the soul ties and emotional baggage that is carried from relationship to relationship. What people don't understand is that not giving yourself the necessary time to replenish your thoughts, you constantly push yourself away from that gift that God wants to give you in relationships.

I often hear several conversations or get asked several questions from people pertaining to things that constantly happen to them in this area. It's generally a "WHY" question, "Why does this keep happening to me?" The answers that some of these individuals receive from their friends or close ones are hilarious. But the answer is simple, a person has not given themselves the time needed to be restored or replenished emotionally. So these things cause a person to have distorted thinking and cloudy judgment in a lot of areas when trying to find someone that want devalue their time in dating and relationship. They have not taken the proper precaution needed to "Get over past hurts." So, they fall victim to what they have been dealing with in the past. I can truly attest to this as well. Because it wasn't until I took the time needed to figure out why all of my dating experiences and relationships were ending the same, but, most importantly why all of them were all going down the same path, nowhere. I had to figure out why I was falling victim to the same process and categorized as an "Eternal Seeker."

Once people detached themselves from the feelings and emotions that they have built for a person and truly observe the real in a person's intentions; they would understand and know if

that person is for them and is here to add value to their life. God's Gift in relationships is simply that Adam's rib that is missing from every man in this world. But a lot of women devalue themselves for a rib cage that is not the fit for them. This goes the same for men as well. Both men and women don't understand the severity of this area pertaining to dating and relationships. Understanding your worth, knowing what your role as a man is, not devaluing the most valuable asset you have, and just following the necessary guidelines in this world of dating. Following these steps to having the relationship and dating experience you want would give people more understanding of that path to "God's Gift."